Miss Juanita's Delta Cuisine

Miss Juanita's
Delta Cuisine

Juanita Emily Caldwell

SARTORIS
LITERARY
GROUP

Copyright © 2019 by Sartoris Literary Group

Library of Congress Control Number: 2019930138

ISBN: 978-1-941644-56-0

Cover Photo: courtesy Juanita Caldwell

All food photos courtesy of Susan Richardson, except for the Frozen French Pastry image, which was taken by Christiana Dickerson.

SARTORIS LITERARY GROUP
Metro-Jackson, Mississippi
www.sartorisliterary.com

To my wonderful family,

past, present and future

FOREWORD

As a young child growing up in Itawamba County, Mississippi, in the 1920s and early 1930s, Juanita Turner started reading books at an early age. Her favorite author was Zane Grey, who was still writing books at the time. She eagerly awaited the arrival of new books, word of which always came when the local librarian called to let her know the library had received his latest book. Thrilled by his tales of adventure, she even toyed with the notion of someday becoming a writer herself, encouraged perhaps by the fact that her grandfather, Steve Turner, who lived just down the road, had helped write the Mississippi Constitution of 1890.

The Great Depression dampened her literary dreams somewhat as it curtailed the book pipeline into Mississippi. New books were hard to come by, not to mention food and clothing. Disaster struck in the late 1930s when her father's two department stores, one in Fulton, the other in Alabama, disappeared almost overnight: one was burned to the ground by an arsonist, the other was robbed by criminals in large trucks who cleaned out the merchandise late one night as the family slept.

The only job that her father could find was as a prison warden at Parchman Farm, Mississippi's notorious state penitentiary located in the Mississippi Delta. As a result, Miss Juanita, her father and mother, and her two brothers and two sisters packed up their belongings and moved into prison housing at a time when it was bursting at the seams with new arrivals, among them Elvis Presley's father, Vernon, who was sent to Parchman Farm in 1938 for forging a four-dollar check to purchase a hog to feed his family. Miss Juanita has no recollections of Presley, but her father likely did. One can only imagine how he felt. His life had been ruined by criminals and now he was charged with keeping in line some of the worst criminals in Mississippi.

Miss Juanita rode the school bus each day from Parchman Farm to Drew High School, from which she was graduated in 1938, the year of

Presley's arrival at the prison. In the early 1940s, the family moved to Greenville, Mississippi. In nearby Leland lived her cousin Hilton Waits, a lawyer who also had earned a master's degree in political science from the University of Mississippi. At the time they arrived in Greenville, Hilton Waits had been serving in the Mississippi House of Representatives for nearly a decade. Later, he served as *Speaker of the House pro tem*.

Miss Juanita's dream of becoming a writer was put on the back burner in the 1940s when she met James L. Dickerson of Virginia, who was serving in the U.S. Army Air Corps. During World War II. When they met, he was stationed at the air base in Greenville. They were married and had a son, James L. Dickerson, Jr., and five years later a daughter, Susan Dickerson.

Miss Juanita survived the loss of her first husband, James L. Dickerson, who died in a boating accident in the early 1950s, and she raised two children as a single mother while living in Hollandale, Mississippi—the daughter ending up teaching nursing and the son ending up working for some of the South's best newspapers and writing more than 30 books—only to later survive the cancer death of her second husband, Dick Caldwell, a retired World War II U.S. Army captain and businessman …. all the time collecting recipes for meals that were prepared while living daily life in the heart of the Mississippi Delta.

Although her ancestors were Presbyterians who had fled religious persecution in Scotland, arriving in America in 1688, Miss Juanita went against family tradition and joined the Hollandale Baptist Church. She returned to her family's Presbyterian roots in the mid-2000s when she relocated to Rankin County and began attending the Lakeside Evangelical Presbyterian Church.

Early on, she saw the value of telling her story through the recipes she collected. Her book offers a walk through Mississippi Delta culinary history that spans eight decades. It also fulfills the dream Miss Juanita nurtured for so many years to become a writer. Now, at age 97, she finally has a book of her own.—**James L. Dickerson**

In the beginning . . .

My mother Rada Kinard, second from right, and her mother,
father and two siblings

CONTENTS

CASSEROLES

I made eye contact with the president and . . .

President Franklin D. Roosevelt visiting my hometown
of Tupelo, Mississippi in 1934 to celebrate the first TVA city.
I was 13 at the time and in the crowd to welcome him.
Photo courtesy Tennessee Valley Authority

. . . he smiled and waved

Sweet Potato Casserole

3 cups cooked, mashed sweet potatoes
½ cup milk
½ cup margarine
½ teaspoon vanilla
½ teaspoon cinnamon

Beat together all of the above ingredients
Put in greased casserole dish

Top with mixture of:
1 cup brown sugar
1/3 cup melted margarine
1/3 cup flour
1 cup chopped nuts

Cook at 350 degrees for 25 minutes.

Variation:
Instead of brown sugar and nuts topping, you can top with marshmallows and cook until brown. Great side dish for holiday dinners that feature dressing or chicken or turkey.

Brunch Casserole

1 dozen boiled eggs
11/2 lb. sausage, cooked, not browned
2 cans cheese soup
1 cup milk
English muffins

Cover 9 x 13 baking dish with cooked sausage, next sprinkle eggs over sausage. Mix cheese soup and milk. Heat until hot. Pour over eggs and sausage. Bake at 350 degrees until it bubbles (about 30 minutes) and serve over English muffins. Serve baked fruit and cheese grits with this.

Yellow Squash Casserole

1 lb. yellow squash
1 large onion
1 stick of margarine
½ cup milk
1 teaspoon sugar
Salt and pepper to taste
1 cup soda crackers crushed
Few drops Tabasco sauce

Cool squash and onion together. Drain well and mash. Then add all the other ingredients, cheese last.

Pour in greased baking dish and sprinkle with flour.

Sprinkle with garlic powder and parmesan cheese. Then add buttered cracker crumbs.

Bake at 300 degrees for 1 hour.

Hash Brown Potato Casserole

1 32 oz. package southern style frozen hash brown potatoes, thawed.
1 pint sour cream
1 can cream of chicken soup, undiluted
½ cup chopped onions, sautéed in ¾ cup margarine, melted
10 ounces sharp cheddar cheese, grated
1 teaspoon salt
½ teaspoon black pepper

Stir well and pour into 9 x 13 casserole. Top with buttered bread crumbs. Bake 50 minutes at 350 degrees.

Spinach Casserole

2 packages frozen chopped spinach
½ teaspoon black pepper
2 teaspoon margarine
¾ teaspoon celery salt
2 tablespoons flour
½ teaspoon salt
2 tablespoons grated onion
1 teaspoon Worcestershire Sauce
½ cup Pet Milk
6 oz. jalapeno cheese
½ cup of liquid from spinach
¾ teaspoon garlic salt

Cook spinach as directed; drain and save liquid.

Melt margarine, stir in flour, Pet milk, vegetable liquid and onion. Cook over low heat until medium thick. Add cheese cut into small pieces until melted. Add all seasonings until smooth. Stir in spinach, mix well.

Butter casserole dish and pour in mixture.

Top with buttered cracker crumbs.

Bake at 350 degrees for 20-30 minutes.

This recipe makes 1 large or 2 small casseroles.

**My father Audie Turner, son of Steve Turner,
who helped write the Mississippi Constitution of 1890.
The photo was taken on his first trip to New York City**

Shoe Peg Corn Casserole

1 can cream of celery soup
1 tablespoon celery flakes
1 tablespoon onion flakes
½ can grated cheese
½ pint sour cream
1 can French style beans (drained)
1 can shoe peg corn (drained)

Mix all above and pour into greased casserole dish.
Top with buttered bread crumbs.
Bake at 350 degrees for 45 minutes.

(Chris Wilson)

Breakfast Casserole

10 slices bread
1 lb. cheddar cheese, grated
1 stick butter, melted
4 cups milk
1 lb. bacon, fried
8 eggs

Place torn bread in a greased 9 x 13 baking dish. Top with crumbled bacon. Combine milk and eggs and beat slightly. Add cheese Pour over bread mixture.

Let stand one hour or maybe do it the night before—and refrigerate. Bake uncovered at 450 degrees for 35-40 minutes.

When Daddy had a big sale …

My father's store in Fulton, MS

… people came from all over

Asparagus Casserole

1 #2 can asparagus, drained
3 hard-boiled eggs
1 cup milk
2 tablespoons flour
1/8 teaspoon Tabasco
¼ teaspoon salt
1 cup grated cheese
Buttered bread crumbs
2 tablespoons margarine

Make sauce with milk, flour, salt and margarine. Cook slowly until thickened. Add cheese. In greased dish layer first thin layer of bread crumbs and add asparagus, chopped eggs, white sauce, then repeat. Top with bread crumbs.

Bake at 350 degrees until hot and bubbly.

Eggplant Casserole

1 medium eggplant
2 tablespoons butter
2 tablespoons of flour
1 cups of milk
2 teaspoons of grated onion
1 cup grated cheese
1 tablespoon catsup
¾ cup soft bread crumbs
2 eggs, with egg whites separated
Salt, pepper and cayenne

Lightly grease the dish. Peel eggplant and cook in salted water, draining thoroughly. Then mash. Make a cream sauce with butter, flour, egg yoks, and milk. Add all ingredients, folding in the egg whites last. Bake at 350 degrees for 45 minutes.

I am on the front row, fourth from the left, with my
co-workers at a Greenville, Miss., bank. It was my first job.

Left to right, my brother Rex, me, my sisters Aileen and Marcelle
during a family get together in Hollandale, MS

Zucchini Pie

2 cups shredded zucchini
¾ cup shredded cheese
1 small chopped onion
¾ cup biscuit mix
½ teaspoon salt
¼ teaspoon pepper
¼ teaspoon sage
¼ cup olive oil
2 eggs lightly beaten

Stir ingredients and pour into a 9 inch pie place. Bake at 350 degrees for 45 minutes. Cool 10 minutes before serving.

Jim's Rockin'
Vegetarian Baked Beans

1 large can Bush's Vegetarian Beans
1 onion, chopped into small pieces
1 bell pepper, chopped into small pieces
3 tablespoons dark brown sugar
1 tablespoon maple syrup

Mix all ingredients in a ceramic baking dish.
Bake at 350 degrees for 1 hour.
Twice as good when re-heated the following day.

(James L. Dickerson)

Plantation Casserole

2 cups chopped cooked chicken, ham or beef
1 cup cooked peas, drained
1 17-ounce container cream corn
¼ lb. cubed American cheese
¼ cup chopped onion
½ cup evaporated milk
1 tablespoon Worcestershire

Combine ingredients and pour into greased 8-inch square baking dish.

Bake at 400 degrees for 10 minutes.

Then top with the following:

1 cup biscuit mix
½ cup cornmeal
1 tablespoons sugar
½ teaspoon salt
1 egg, beaten
½ cup milk

Pour batter around the edge of the baking dish, leaving the center uncovered.

Bake an additional 20 minutes.

My mother and father, Audie and Rada Turner

Chicken Divan (Broccoli)

4 chicken breasts
1 tablespoon margarine
2 packages frozen broccoli
2 cans cream of chicken soup
1 cup mayonnaise
1 teaspoon lemon juice
¼ cup buttered bread crumbs

Cook chicken till tender and cut in bite-sized pieces. Cook broccoli for 5 minutes, drain, and spread in greased casserole dish, then add chicken.

Mix soup, mayonnaise and lemon juice, then pour over chicken. Top with buttered bread crumbs.

Bake at 350 degrees for 30minutes.

Ham Casserole

1 ½ cups chopped ham
1 5-ounce package small egg noodles
1 tablespoon each dried onion, pepper, and parsley
1 can cream of mushroom soup
1 can cream of cheddar cheese soup
1 cup buttered bread crumbs

Put dried onion, pepper and parsley into a casserole dish with both cans of soup (undiluted.) Stir, adding the chopped ham until the meat appears evenly dispersed. Bake in 300 degree oven for about an hour (covered).

Cook egg noodles according to instructions on package. Drain and add the soup mixture and top with buttered bread crumbs. Bake at 350 degrees until the mixture browns.

Summer Squash Casserole

6 cups sliced yellow squash
¼ cup chopped onion
1 can cream of chicken soup
1 cup sour cream
1 cup shredded carrots
1 8-oz. package herb stuffing mix
1/2 cup margarine, melted

Cook squash and onion in water to cover about 5 minutes. Drain well. Combine soup and sour cream. Stir in carrots, squash and onion.

In a separate bowl combine stuffing mix with margarine and spread half of this mix in 9 x 13 baking dish.

Spoon vegetable mixture on top and sprinkle with remainder of stuffing mix. Bake at 350 for 30 minutes.

Serves 6 to 8.

(**Gladys Thompson**, my sister-in-law)

My son James eating his favorite dish, Hot Tamale Pie

Hot Tamale Pie

1 large onion (chopped)
1½ pounds ground beef
2 cans condensed tomato soup, 1 can of water
1 teaspoon salt
1/4 teaspoon black pepper
3 heaping tablespoons chili powder
3/4 cup chopped black olives
3/4 cup whole kernel corn

TOPPING
1 cup corn meal (self-rising)
1/2 stick margarine
1 egg
1/4 teaspoon baking soda
¾ cup buttermilk or milk

Add enough milk to make soft batter.

Brown onion and meat in 1 tablespoon hot oil. Add remaining ingredients. Pour in greased 8 x 8 deep-dish casserole dish, cover and bake at 325 degrees for 1 1/2 hours.

Add topping.

Bake, uncovered, for about 25 minutes.

Best when served with baked potato and/or green salad.

My 1938 class photo, top row center, from
my senior year at Drew (MS) High School

SIDE DISHES

My husband James L. Dickerson and I in the 1940s

Acorn Squash

1 acorn squash
1 teaspoon margarine or butter
1 tablespoon maple syrup (or brown sugar or honey)

Preheat oven to 375 degrees

Line a baking sheet with aluminum foil. Cut squash in half. Remove seeds and place cut side down on the baking sheet.

Bake for 30 minutes or until squash is soft. Remove from the oven and turn the oven to broil

Turn squash cut side up. Mix melted margarine/butter and maple syrup in a small bowl. Brush over the flesh of the squash and fill the center cavity with maple syrup, honey or brown sugar) Broil for 5 minutes or until squash begins to brown.

Remove from oven and serve.

(**Ina Dickerson**)

Rice Consommé

1 cup of rice
1 can of beef consommé
1 can French onion soup
1 stick of margarine or butter melted

Mix all ingredients.

Bake in 2 quart covered dish at 350 degrees for about 1 hour.

Corn Pudding

2 cans creamed corn
1 stick margarine or butter, melted
1 tablespoon flour
2 tablespoons sugar
½ teaspoon salt
4 eggs, beaten
1 cup milk

Mix all together, pour in 2 quart greased casserole.

Bake at 350 degrees for 50 minutes or until knife inserted is clean.

Sausage Balls

1 package Kraft sharp cheese
1 lb. hot sausage
3 cups Bisquick

Melt cheese in double boiler.

Stir in sausage and add Bisquick into the mixture by hand.

Then shape into small balls.

Place on greased pan.

Bake at 350 degrees about 10 minutes

My husband James L Dickerson

Potato Salad

3 medium potatoes
3 hard-boiled eggs
Chopped sweet pickles to taste
1 teaspoon French's mustard
Mayonnaise to taste (about 4 tablespoons)
Salt and pepper to taste

Peel, cube, and boil potatoes until soft when probed with fork. Drain and set aside. Gently mix all ingredients in serving dish. Sprinkle with paprika. Cover and put in the refrigerator.

Spinach Dip

1 package frozen chopped spinach
1 cup sour cream
1 cup mayonnaise
1 small can water chestnuts, drained and chopped
1 package Knorr Swiss vegetable soup mix (dry)
1 tablespoon chopped onion, sautéed

Cook spinach as directed on package, drain well.

Mix all ingredients. Refrigerate 24 hours.

(My sister **Marcelle Young**)

My older sister Marcelle Young

Verne's Shrimp Dip

1 small onion (grated)
½ cup Ketchup
1 cup mayonnaise

Mix all of the above, then add:
1 Tablespoon Worcestershire Sauce
½ cup salad oil
1 Tablespoon paprika
Dash of hot sauce

(use a small amount of garlic if desired.)

Mix well and refrigerate.

Sweet Potato Balls

2 cups cooked mashed sweet potatoes
1/3 cup brown Sugar
½ teaspoon grated orange rind
3 tablespoons orange juice
8 marshmallows or more
1 cup flaked coconut

In bowl combine the first 4 ingredients.
Shape potatoes around each marshmallow, roll in coconut. Place on baking sheet. Bake at 350 degrees for 15-20 minutes. Serves 8 or more.
   (**Gladys Thompson**, my sister-in-law)

My granddaughter Jennifer with my Spicy Crackers

Spicy Country Store Crackers

12 to 16 ounces of crackers
½ teaspoon dill weed
¼ teaspoon lemon pepper
¼ teaspoon garlic powder
1 envelope Hidden Valley Ranch salad dressing (dry mix, with no buttermilk)

\Whisk together all the ingredients and pour over crackers.

Place a cookie sheet in 275 degree oven for 15 to 20 minutes.

Cool, then store in air-tight container.

Mrs. Caldwell's Chili Sauce

24 ripe tomatoes
6 green peppers
4 cups sugar
1 tablespoon all-spice, cloves and nutmeg
8 onions
8 cups vinegar
4 tablespoons salt

Put tomatoes in boiling water and remove skins. Cut up all ingredients and simmer together for about 2 hours. Put in jars and seal while hot.

My granddaughter Janet loves my Levee Party Mix

Levee Party Mix

2 cups corn Chex
2 cups rice Chex
2 cups wheat Chex
2 cups Honey Nut Cherrios
1 cup nuts

Seasonings:
½ cup margarine, melted
1 ¼ teaspoon salt
1 teaspoon garlic powder
1 teaspoon onion powder
1 teaspoon chili powder
½ teaspoon hot pepper sauce
2 tablespoons Worcestershire Sauce

Mix all seasonings. Mix all Chex and nuts. Put in large flat pan and pour seasonings over ingredients. Bake at 250 degrees for 1 hour, stirring every 15 minutes. When done, spread on absorbent paper until cool.

Broccoli and Peppers

2 lbs. broccoli
2 tablespoons butter
4 green onions, chopped
½ red pepper, chopped
Juice of one lemon
1 teaspoon salt
¼ teaspoon of black pepper

Cook broccoli in salted water until crisp. Melt butter and then add onions and red peppers. Cook uncovered, adding lemon juice, salt and black pepper. Drain broccoli and toss with the butter-and-peppers mixture.

(My sister **Marcelle Young**)

Cucumber Pickles

Use fresh, firm medium cucumbers. Wash and cut them into sticks. Pour boiling water over them and let stand overnight. Next morning, pack solidly linto clean jars.

Make solution of:

3 ¾ cups vinegar
3 cups sugar
3 tablespoons salt
4 ½ teaspoons celery seed
3 ½ teaspoons tumerac
3 teaspoons mustard seed

Boil for 5 minutes. Pour boiling hot over cucumbers in jars. Put on caps, screwing band tight. Process in boiling water bath for 5 minutes.

Solution fills 6 pint jars.

If sweeter pickle is desired double amount of sugar.

Susan's Shrimp Dip

1 cup mayonnaise
1/3 cup chili sauce
1 small onion, chopped
2 dashes of Worcestershire Sauce
Juice from 1 lemon
Small amount of horseradish
Dash of Tabasco

Mix all ingredients, and use last 2 ingredients to suit your own taste.

Dill Potatoes

10 medium potatoes, boiled, peeled and diced
4 dill pickles, chopped
1 can pimento, chopped

Combine all ingredients and put in buttered casserole and cover with sauce:

1 stick margarine
½ lb. old cheese
2 cups milk
½ teaspoon salt
1 tablespoon steak sauce
2 cups milk
½ teaspoon salt
¼ teaspoon pepper
½ teaspoon dry mustard

Melt margarine in double boiler. Add remaining ingredients and stir until smooth. Pour over potatoes and bake at 350 degrees for 1 hour.

(My sister **Marcelle Young**)

Ro-Tel Cheese Dip

1 box Velveeta cheese
1 can Ro-Tel tomatoes

Mix together in double boiler until cheese is melted.

Turn heat on low to keep dip warm for dipping.

Philly Brunch Quiche

1 8-ounce package cream cheese, cubed
1 cup milk
4 eggs, beaten
¼ cup chopped onions (sautéed)
1 tablespoon margarine
1 cup finely chopped ham
¼ cup chopped pimento
¼ teaspoon dill weed
Dash of pepper

Pastry for 1 10-inch pie crust. Cook at 400 degrees for 12-15 minutes. Combine milk and cream cheese in sauce pan, on low heat until smooth, then add all other ingredients and pour in pastry shell. Bake at 350 degrees for 35-40 minutes or until set. Variation: 1 package chopped cooked spinach, drained.

Fried Cucumbers

3 or 4 medium cucumbers
1 cup of milk
1 egg
½ teaspoon salt
1 cup of all-purpose flour
Enough vegetable oil to cover bottom of pan

First peel the cucumbers, cutting into finger-sized lengths. Scrape the seeds off. Then beat the ingredients into a lump-free batter. Take each cucumber finger and dip into flour, then into the batter, making sure it is well coated. Then place into a medium-hot deep frying pan until brown, turning only once to twice. Once brown place on fold paper towel to that the cucumbers can drain. Serves 4.

(James L. Dickerson)

Here I am, center, with my father and my dog Prince
at Parchman Farm. You can see some of the inmates
in the background. I was sixteen at the time.

Cornbread Dressing

This was my mother's dressing and was probably passed on to her from her mother. The earliest I remember eating it was in the 1930s. Certainly, we enjoyed it at Thanksgiving and Christmas when we lived on the grounds of Parchman Farm.

1 pan of cornbread, crumbled (recipe below)
8 slices of loaf bread, torn in pieces
2 onions and 1 cup of celery, both finely chopped
1 teaspoon salt
1 teaspoon black pepper
1 teaspoon sage
1 cans chicken broth
1 can cream of chicken soup
2 eggs, beaten

Sauté all ingredients. If more liquid is needed, use more broth. The mixture needs to be sloppy, but not soupy. Pour in pans and bake at 350 degrees for about 1 hour.

(**Rada Kinard Turner**, my mother)

Cornbread

2 cups self-rising corn meal
¼ cup Crisco oil
½ teaspoon salt
2 eggs

Mix with milk to make a sloppy mixture. Pour in greased pan, cook at 400 degrees until light brown. Cool.

(This is my recipe for cornbread)

Brown Sugar Glazed Carrots

1 lb. baby carrots
2 tablespoons of butter or margarine
1/3 cup brown sugar
Dash of salt
Pepper, if wanted
1 cup water

Combine baby carrots with other ingredients in a medium pan. Stir to blend the ingredients. Bring to a fast boil. Lower heat to medium and continue with boiling for about 20 minutes or until carrots are tender.

Wild Rice Stuffing

1 cup wild rice
¼ cup butter
¼ chopped onion
1 can consommé
2 cups water
¼ teaspoon salt
½ cup stale bread crumbs

Sautee rice and onions in the butter, slowly heating

Once rice turns yellow, stir in the remaining ingredients.

Cover and simmer for 1 ¼ hours, or until all the moisture is absorbed (as an alternative you could bake the mixture in a covered casserole dish for around 1½ hours. This stuffing can be enjoyed as a side dish or stuffed into a duck or chicken or even green peppers.

(My son **James L. Dickerson**)

Mac & Cheese with Sausage

6-8 pre-cooked port sausages
1 package (7 ounces) elbow macaroni
2 tablespoons margarine
2 tablespoons all-purpose flour
½ cup non-fat milk
¼ teaspoon cayenne or black pepper
2 cups low-fat shredded cheese
½ chopped onion
¼ cup diced pimento

Lightly brown the pre-cooked sausage and set aside.

Cook macaroni according to package instructions. Melt the margarine in a saucepan over medium heat and add the flour. Cook for 1 minute, stirring every 10 seconds or so.

Add milk and continue cooking until the mixture is thickened and smooth.

Add pimento, chopped onion, and cayenne or black pepper.

Reduce heat to low and add cheese. Continue cooking until the cheese melts, stirring occasionally.

Add drained macaroni and sausage (crumbled into small pieces).

Pour into an oven dish and bake for 15 minutes at 325 degrees.

(My son **James L. Dickerson**)

My older brother Harold at war in the South Pacific
He died shortly after returning home
of disease contracted in the South Pacific

BREAD

Homemade Sourdough Bread

Sourdough Bread

To make homemade Sourdough bread you will need to obtain a "live" starter either from a friend who bakes, or from the Internet. Amazon offers a variety of starters. Once you obtain a starter you will have to "feed" it on a regular basis.

Starter Feed:
¾ cups sugar
1 cup warm water
3 tablespoons instant potatoes

Mix and add to starter every 5 days

Bread:
¼ cup sugar
6 cups Pillsbury bread flour
½ cup corn oil
1 ½ warm water
1 tablespoon salt
1 cup starter

Mix sugar, oil and water, then add starter, flour and salt. Keep starter in refrigerator: on 5th day feed (day of feeding is Day 1) Leave out of refrigerator for 8 to 12 hours.

Use 1 cup to make bread:
Put dough in a greased bowl, and turn dough over leaving greased side up. Cover with foil and leave out of refrigerator overnight. In the morning punch dough down and divide into three parts. Knead each part on a floured board a few times less than 10.

Put in greased loaf pans and brush tops with oil. Let rise 4 to 5 hours. Bake at 350 degrees for about 20 minutes (or until brown). Remove from pans, Brush tops with butter. Let cool on wire racks before cutting.

My children, Susan and James

Marcelle's Light Rolls

¾ cup warm water
2 cups flour
¾ teaspoon salt
1 package yeast
3 tablespoons sugar
4 tablespoons shortening
1 egg, beaten

Dissolve yeast in warm water. Five minutes later, stir all ingredients together and let rise for about 30 minutes. Spoon into muffin pan, half full. Cover and let rise 30 minutes.

Bake at 425 degrees until brown.

Marcelle's Cheddar Muffins

2 cups all-purpose flour
3 ½ teaspoons baking powder
½ teaspoon salt
1 teaspoon paprika
1 cup shredded cheddar cheese
1 egg, beaten
1 cup milk
¼ cup melted butter

Combine first 5 ingredients in large bowl, Make a well in the center for the mixture.

Combine egg, milk and butter and add to dry ingredients, stirring until moistened. Spoon into greased muffin pans, filling 2/3 full. Bake at 425 degrees for 20 minutes..

Remove from pans immediately after taking from oven.

Marcelle's Spoon Rolls

1 package dry yeast
2 cups warm water
½ cup sugar
1 egg, slightly beaten
½ cup cooking oil
1 teaspoon salt
4 cups self-rising flour

Dissolve yeast in warm water. Add all the other ingredients and beat until well mixed. Store in refrigerator in air-tight container until ready to use. Spoon to greased muffin tins. Bake at 400 degrees for 20 minutes.

Three generations: my father, my husband James, and my son James on the levee in Greenville, MS

Walk on the Wild Side

Bushy-Tail Squirrel 'n' Dumplings

Squirrels are plentiful in the Mississippi Delta, both in the towns and in the big forests. Squirrel hunting has long been a Delta tradition, whether they are harvested with a .22 rifle or a small bore shotgun.

There are three squirrel seasons in Mississippi: May 15 to June 1 for spring squirrel; September 24 to 30 for youth squirrel; and October 1 to February 28 for fall squirrel. Apparently, the only times Mississippi squirrels get a breather are during the months of March, April, July and August. That pretty much eliminates any squirrel hunting on Confederate Memorial Day.

 As they say, cleaning squirrels for the dumplin' pan is not for sissies. It involves skinning the animal, gutting it properly, and cutting and snapping off its appendages. If you are not expert at this, you will want to find someone who is. Therein lies the secret to making squirrel and dumplin's.

Because the meaty portions of a squirrel are its legs that should be the focus of your efforts. Some people throw the head into the dumplin' mix, but we never found that to be an appetizing facet of this particular cuisine.

INGREDIENTS
3-4 squirrels
2 cups all-purpose flour
1quart water / 1 quart chicken broth
2 ½ teaspoons of salt
½ teaspoon baking soda
¾ cup of buttermilk
3 tablespoons of vegetable shortening

Place squirrel meat in a pot of boiling water and chicken broth. Add salt. Bring to a boil and cover, reducing heat to medium low. Cook for about one hour.

Once cooked, remove the squirrel meat from broth and allow to cool until it can be handled and cut into bite-sized pieces.

As the squirrel meat is cooling, combine the flour and baking soda into a large bowl, blending in the shortening with your fingers until it resembles a coarse meal. Then add the buttermilk and stir until the dry ingredients are moist.

Place the resulting dough on the counter and knead 4 or 5 times. Shape the dough into balls the size you are accustomed to seeing with spaghetti. Small dumplings are not as tasty.

Drop the balls into boiling broth and reduce heat to low and cook until the dough balls are of desired consistency (about 10 minutes).

Stir in the squirrel meat and add black pepper. The resulting meal will not be nearly as white as chicken and dumplins' but it will scamper all up and down your taste buds.

Wild Doves

8-12 plucked and cleaned dove breasts
Celery salt
Garlic salt
Black pepper
Juice of 1 lemon
Salt
1 can mushrooms
Curry powder
3 teaspoons Worcestershire sauce.

Dip each dove in oil, place in Dutch oven, sprinkle not so generously with dry mustard and pepper, add mushrooms with juice and enough water to make ½ inch liquid on bottom of roaster. Cover and cook at 250 degrees for 2 ½ hours. Add lemon and Worcestershire and cook 14 minutes more.

(My sister **Marcelle Young**)

Fried Bluegill Bream or White Perch

First use a sharp knife to descale the fish. Then remove the head and tail. Using the knife, proceed to debone and then fillet the fish, being careful not to allow to remain in the fillet. Beat 2-4 eggs in a bowl and coat both sides of each fillet. Next fill a plastic bag with finely crush bread crumbs or croutons. Drop each fillet, one at a time, into the bag and shake until it appears the fillet is well coated. Now you are ready to drop each fillet into a large iron frying pan to which you have added vegetable or olive oil. The pan should be hot when you add the fillets. Lift the fillets frequently and check to make sure they are not overcooked. Once one side is golden brown, flip to the other side and cook until it is golden brown. Tasty with iced tea and served with cole slaw, French fries, beans of most any kind, and hush puppies.

(My son **James L. Dickerson**)

Marinated Roast Venison

5 lb. venison roast, trimmed of all fat
6-8 strips of bacon

Marinade:
½ cup vinegar
3 cups water
1 cup apple juice
3 tablespoons sugar
½ teaspoon salt
¼ teaspoon pepper
½ cup chopped onion
1 clove garlic, crushed
4 orange slices

Place roast in a bowl. Mix all the marinade ingredients and pour over the meat. Cover and allow to chill in the refrigerator for 24 hours, taking care to turn the meat every couple of hours, if possible (you don't have to stay up all night to do this).

Before you cook the roast, drain the meat and pat dry. However, put the marinade aside and save it.

Place the meat in a shallow pan and cover with bacon. Roast at 325 degrees for 30 minutes, then start basting every 10 minutes or so with the marinade you have kept heated. Allow 25 minutes per pound of venison.

This recipe should serve 8.

(My son **James L. Dickerson**)

Nana's Fried Quail

6 Delta or Hill Country quail, cleaned and cut lengthwise down the center, separating the breast from the thigh
1 cup buttermilk
1 cup all-purpose flour
¼ teaspoon salt
¼ teaspoon pepper
Vegetable oil for frying

Combine the dry ingredients in a bowl.

In a separate bowl, pour the buttermilk.

Place each quail half in the bowl of buttermilk and turn to coat. Then place the buttermilk-coated quail into the bowl of dry ingredients and turn to coat. Shake off any excess flour and transfer the quail to a sheet pan. When completed for all quail pieces, refrigerate for no more than 1 hour.

Pour the vegetable oil into a large saucepan or skillet to a depth of at 2 to 3 inches and heat on medium heat until the oil is bubbling. Then transfer the quail to the saucepan or skillet and check for browning on the bottom, turning when it is golden brown.

Repeat the process for the top side of the quail. Be careful not to overheat and burn. Once cooked, remove and place the quail either on a raised rack or a plate covered with white paper towels to drain.

(From my son James who liked to sit at the kitchen table and talk to my mother as she cooked meals he thought were interesting to watch be prepared.)

My daughter Susan and my son James

MEAT DISHES

My daughter Susan with freshly cooked chicken 'n' dumplins'

Chicken 'n' Dumplings

Most European and North American cultures have their own version of chicken and dumplings, but there is only one chicken 'n' dumplins' Delta-style . It is a Depression era creation of the American South. During good times, chickens have been plentiful in the South, so much so that there were usually enough for everyone at a gathering to have a couple pieces of fried chicken, the preferred way of cooking chicken in the South.

During the Great Depression, family or church gatherings were lucky to have a single chicken available to make a meal. Ingenious Southern cooks worked miracles of biblical proportions with that one chicken by boiling it until it was tender enough to fall off the bone and then cutting those pieces into bite-sized portions and stirring them in a milky, somewhat sloppy, concoction of meatball-sized dumplings sufficient to feed a multitude.

My mother first began cooking this dish for us during the Depression when we lived at Parchman Farm (the state penitentiary), which was located in the Delta, so that my father could have a job as a prison warden.

Previously, he had owned two department stores in the Tupelo area, only to have one burned to the ground by an arsonist and the other stripped of all its merchandise by bandits in the dead of night driving large trucks.

INGREDIENTS
2 chicken breasts
2 cups all-purpose flour
1quart water / 1 quart chicken broth
2 ½ teaspoons of salt
½ teaspoon baking soda
¾ cup of buttermilk
3 tablespoons of vegetable shortening

Place chicken in a pot of boiling water and chicken broth. Add salt. Bring to a boil and cover, reducing heat to medium low. Cook for about one hour.

Once cooked, remove chicken from broth and allow to cool until the meat can be handled and cut into bite-sized pieces.

As the chicken is cooling, combine the flour and baking soda into a large bowl, blending in the shortening with your fingers until it resembles a coarse meal. Then add the buttermilk and stir until the dry ingredients are moist.

Place the resulting dough on the counter and knead 4 or 5 times. Shape the dough into balls the size you are accustomed to seeing with spaghetti. Drop the balls into boiling broth and reduce heat to low and cook until the dough balls are of desired consistency (about 10 minutes).

Stir in the chicken and add black pepper. The resulting meal will be white as newly fallen snow.

Poppy Seed Chicken

4 chicken breasts
1 can cream of mushroom soup
1 carton sour cream
1 stick Ritz crackers
½ cup margarine
1 tablespoon poppy seed

Cook chicken and cut in bite-size pieces.

Mix with soup and sour cream.

Spread in 9 x 12 baking dish.

Crumble crackers with margarine.

Top off chicken mixture.

Sprinkle poppy seed on top.

Bake at 350 degrees until hot and bubbly.

(Verne Campbell)

Oven Fried Chicken

4 chicken breast halves
Hellman's mayonnaise
Italian bread crumbs

Brush chicken with mayonnaise. Then shake the chicken in a bag of bread crumbs (one breast at a time). Once the meat is well coated, then place on rack in broiler pan. Bake at 400 degrees for 45 to 60 minutes, or until golden brown.

In 1955 I took James and Susan, and their babysitter Janelle Christopher, to Washington, D.C. I took this picture as we entered the White House. Dwight Eisenhower was president at the time

Baked Chicken Loaf

4 whole chicken breasts
1 tablespoon minced parsley
1 pimento, chopped
½ teaspoon salt / ¼ teaspoon pepper
1 cup milk
2 eggs
2 teaspoons butter, melted
2 cups soft bread crumbs

Combine first 8 ingredients in bowl, add 1¾ cup bread crumbs. Mix well.

Spoon into load pan. Bake at 325 degrees for 45 minutes Cut into squares.

Miss Juanita's Meat Loaf

1 ½ pounds of ground round steak
1 ½ cups bread crumbs
¼ cup warm water
¾ cup ketchup
1 tablespoon Worcestershire Sauce
2 eggs, beaten
1 envelope of onion soup mix
8 oz. tomato sauce

Mix all of the above ingredients.

Shape into a loaf.

Place in a dish and cover.

Bake, covered at 350 degrees for about 1 hour.

Party Chicken

4 whole chicken breasts, skinned and deboned.

4 slices of bacon, wrapped around chicken.

Crumble dried beef in bottom of 9 x 13 baking dish, greased.

Place the chicken in the dish.

Mix 1 can of chicken soup with ¼ cup sour cream and pour over the chicken.

Cover and let sit overnight in the refrigerator.

Next day, bake covered for 2 ½ hours uncovered, Inspect and bake ½ hour longer.

Stuffed Green Peppers

6 large green peppers
1 lb. ground chuck
¾ cup chopped onion
¼ cup chopped green pepper
1 clove garlic crushed
1/3 cup chopped celery
1`17-ounce can of cream style corn
1 teaspoon salt
1/8 teaspoon pepper
Dash of red pepper
½ cup Italian bread crumbs
¼ cup shredded cheddar cheese

Cut off tops of green peppers, remove seeds. Cook peppers 5 minutes in boiling water (salted) and drain. Cook ground beef, onion, pepper, garlic, celery until beef is browned. Drain. Add corn, salt, pepper until heated. Fill green peppers with mixture and put in baking pan. Combine bread crumbs, cheese, and sprinkle over peppers. Bake at 350 degrees for 15 minutes or until brown
(My sister Marcelle Young)

Crispy Baked Catfish

1 lb. catfish fillets
Black pepper
2 tablespoons vegetable oil
1/3 cup corn flake crumbs

Wash and dry fillets and cut into serving pieces. Season and dip into oil and coat with corn flake crumbs.. Arrange in a single layer in a lightly oiled, shallow baking dish. Bake at 475 degrees for 20 minutes without turning.

(Dot Peyton)

Baked Chicken Tenders

8 chicken tenders
4 tablespoon olive oil
4 tablespoons soy sauce
3 teaspoons ginger
2 tablespoons water
1½ orange marmalade

Lay chicken flat in baking dish. Combine all other ingredients, except marmalade. Drizzle ingredients over chicken. Cook covered tightly at 350 degrees for 30 minutes. Turn chicken over and drizzle ingredients on it again. Cook until tender, check often. When done, spoon marmalade over each piece of chicken and cook 5 to 10 minutes longer.

Chicken Wings Pacifica

1 stick margarine or butter
1 cup soy sauce
1 cup brown sugar
¾ cup water
½ teaspoon dry mustard
3 pounds chicken wings (or more—they disappear fast

In a small pot, heat butter or margarine, soy sauce, sugar, water, and mustard until butter and sugar melt. Cool. Arrange wings in shallow baking pan. Pour mixture over wings and marinate at least two hours, turning once or twice. Bake in same pan in a 375-degree oven for 75 to 90 minutes, turning occasionally. Drain on paper towels.

(Actress **Betty White**. My sons James was visiting me once while he was putting together a book of celebrity recipes. While there he received word of this recipe from Betty White. I was thrilled because I was a huge fan of *The Golden Girls*.)

Lasagna

1 lb. ground round beef, browned and drained
Italian meat sauce. I use 1 large Prego, 1 large Ragu
Lasagna noodles (large box, 6 noodles)
12 ounce carton of cottage cheese
1 egg, beaten
1 package mozzarella cheese sliced
Parmesan cheese

Cook noodles, set aside

Layer in 9 x 13 greased pan in this order:

1-sauce, a little in bottom of pan
2-noodles, cover bottom of pan
3-cottage cheese containers (entire container), mixed together
with egg
4-Sauce
5-cheese slices
6-noodles
7-more sauce
8-sprinkle with parmesan cheese

Then back into the oven at 350 degrees for 40 or 45
minutes.

Let sit 15 or 20 minutes before serving.

(Julie Peyton)

Chicken Lasagna Florentine

4 to 6 lasagna noodles
1 10-ounce package of frozen spinach, thawed
2 cups cooked chopped chicken
2 cups shredded cheddar cheese
1 tablespoon minced onion
¼ to ½ teaspoon nutmeg
¼ teaspoon pepper
1 tablespoon soy sauce
1 can cream of mushroom soup
1 8-ouncecarton of sour cream
1/3 cup mayonnaise
1 cup freshly grated parmesan cheese
Butter-pecan topping desired
2 tablespoons margarine
1 cup chopped nuts

Cook noodles, drain and set aside.

Drain spinach well, press between paper towels to absorb remaining moisture.

Combine all ingredients except noodles and parmesan cheese and topping.

Grease 11 x 7 x 1 ½ baking dish. Spread small amount of chicken mixture, then noodles, then chicken mixture. Repeat above and then sprinkle with parmesan cheese.

Bake covered at 350 degrees for 55-60 minutes.

Let stand 15 minutes before serving.

Chicken Loaf

1 4-pound chicken
1 cup cooked rice
2 or 3 cups fresh bread crumbs (loaf bread)
1 teaspoon salt
1 large can mushroom soup
1 cup chicken broth
3 eggs, beaten

Cook chicken until tender and cut into small pieces. Mix with the other ingredients in the order given. Bake slowly for 1 hour in a loaf pan and serve with the following sauce:

2 cups chicken broth
1 cup butter
1 can mushroom soup
1 cup flour
1 teaspoon lemon juice
1 cup cream or milk
Salt and pepper to taste

Blend the flour and cream and add to the butter which has been melted and combined with mushrooms and chicken broth. Cook 5 minutes and serve over loaf.

(My sister **Aileen Goggins**)

Poulet d' Artichoke

2 (14 oz.) cans artichoke hearts
1 teaspoon lemon juice
2 2/3 cups diced, cooked chicken breasts
2 cans cream of chicken soup
1 cup mayonnaise
1 teaspoon curry powder
1 ¾ cups grated sharp cheddar cheese
1 ¼ cups bread crumbs
2 tablespoons butter, melted

Drain artichoke and spread in a 9 x 13 casserole dish. Spread chicken on top.

Combine the soup, mayonnaise, lemon juice and curry powder and pour over chicken.

Sprinkle with cheese.

Toss bread crumbs with butter and place on top.

Bake at 350 degrees for 25 minutes.

Serves 8.

My father, Audie Turner, and I at C.R. Anthony's in Hollandale
He was manager of the store for more than three decades
and when he retired I followed in his footsteps for a time
before returning to my banking career at Bank of Hollandale

Chicken Ro-Tel

5 chicken breast halves
1 large green pepper
2 medium onions
1 cup chopped celery
1½ stick margarine
1 can Ro-Tel tomatoes
1 12-ounce vermicelli noodles
2 lbs. Velvetta cheese, cubed
1 16-ounce petit English peas
Salt and pepper to taste
2 tablespoons Worcestershire sauce
1/8 tablespoon Tabasco sauce

Bake chicken in foil until tender and cut into small pieces.
Save liquid and set aside. Finely chop pepper, onions and
celery and then sauté them in margarine. Mash Ro-Tel
tomatoes with for. Chop cheese into small cubes

Place in large container to mix and then cook and drain the
noodles, saving the liquid. Pour hot noodles, sautéed celery,
onions and peppers over cheese to melt. Stir in Ro-Tel
tomatoes, chicken, seasonings and peas, drained.

Add canned chicken broth if extra liquid is needed. You want
the mixture to be sloppy but not soupy.

Spoon into greased baking dishes.
Sprinkle with garlic powder, then grated parmesan cheese
and top with buttered cracker crumbs.

Cook at 400 degrees for about 30 minutes.

(**Kay Ingram**)

Orange Chicken Tenders

2 tablespoons vegetable oil or olive oil
2 teaspoons soy sauce
1 ½ teaspoons ginger
1 tablespoon water
¾ teaspoons garlic powder
Chicken tenders
Orange marmalade

Combine:

Oil, soy sauce, ginger, water and garlic powder and drizzle over the chicken tenders.

Cook covered at 350 degrees for 30 minutes. Turn chicken over and cook an additional 30 minutes.

Add marmalade on each piece of chicken and cook covered for 5 to 10 minutes.

SALADS

In Hollandale, on our way to church

Deer Creek
Chicken Salad

4 to 5 cups baked chicken, chopped.
2 cups celery, finely chopped.
8 hard-boiled eggs, finely mashed.
1 cup sweet pickle relish.

Add to first four ingredients:
Chicken broth
Mayonnaise, measure by sight.
½ teaspoon salt and pepper.
Enough paprika to decorate the top
1 teaspoon lemon juice.

Add broth and mayonnaise sparingly and slowly.

Salad will firm as it chills.

Tip: I taste as I combine the ingredients.

My son James, left, and my daughter, Susan, second from right, with Suzanne Peyton, Baily Peyton, Gay Gill and Charlie Wilson

Tuna Salad

1 can good tuna, drained
2 hard-boiled eggs, cooled and mashed
1 medium apple, peeled and grated
2 or 3 sweet pickles, finely chopped
Add mayonnaise to taste

Mix all ingredients and spoon in serving dish. Sprinkle paprika on top

Keep in refrigerator

Dump Fruit Salad

1 can sliced peaches (15 ounce), drained
1 can mandarin orange slices (15 ounce)
1 can chunky pineapple (15 ounce), drained
1 box strawberry pie filling (15 ounce)
3 large bananas, sliced

Combine all the ingredients except bananas and chill a few hours.

Just before serving, fold in sliced bananas.

This is good with a fruit salad topping.

Ambrosia

Ambrosia

10 to 12 large navel oranges (sweet)
1 16-ounce can crushed pineapple
Coconut (12 ounce or 14 ounce) at least
½ cup sugar

Peel and cut up oranges in very small bite size pieces.

Drain pineapple and add to oranges and mix, holding juice in reserve.

Add pineapple juice and mix.

Add coconut and mix.

Add sugar (1/4 cup at a time and no more than ½ cup total).

Cover and refrigerate until ready to serve.

Pistachio Salad

1 box pistachio pudding mix
1 large can crushed pineapple (do not drain)
8 or 9 ounce carton Cool Whip
2 cups miniature marshmallows
1 cup chopped nuts

Dissolve pudding mix with pineapple and juice.

Add all other ingredients.

This can be served after chilled or it can be frozen

Very Berry Salad

Greens

1-2 heads of Romaine Lettuce or the box of baby romaine
lettuce
Fresh broccoli flowers (no stems: 2-3 cups)
Green onions chopped very thin (1 stem)
Fresh carrots (½ to 1 cup)

Clean and pat dry lettuce; break into bite-size pieces. Wash
and cut broccoli into very small "flowers". Do not use the
stems. Add onions and carrots. Set aside.

Crunch

1 package uncooked Ramen Noodles (discard flavor pack)
broken into small pieces
1 cup chopped pecans
½ stick of butter

Melt butter in heavy skillet: sauté dry noodles and chopped
pecans until toasted, stirring constantly. It browns fast, so do
not let it burn. Remove from heat and spread on paper towel
to cool.

Dressing

1 cup canola oil
1 cup Splenda or sugar
¾ cup red wine vinegar
3 tablespoons soy sauce

1½ teaspoons black pepper
(I add a handful of dried cranberries to the dressing)

Combine ingredients. It needs to sit for a little while before serving.

Fruit

Fresh strawberries
Fresh blueberries
Fresh raspberries
Grapes
Mandarin oranges (drained)

Combine fruit and set aside. Just before serving, combine greens, fruit, crunch and dressing. It gets soggy fast. Just use enough dressing to get everything wet, not too much.

(Mardi Allen)

Fruit Salad Dressing

½ cup sugar
2 tablespoons flour
1 egg
1 cup pineapple juice
1 tablespoon butter
1 cup whipped topping

Mix and cook on stovetop in a sauce pan, stirring often, until thick. Then fold in the whipped topping and chill.

My daughter the nurse

DESSERTS

Dick Caldwell and I at my daughter Susan's wedding

Amalgamation Cake

6 large eggs
2 teaspoons baking soda
1 cup all-purpose flour
2 teaspoons baking soda
1 cup butter
2 teaspoons nutmeg
2 cups sugar
2 teaspoons cinnamon
2 cups blackberry jam
1 teaspoon cloves
6 tablespoons buttermilk
1 cup black walnuts

Cream butter and sugar, then add eggs, one at a time, beating well after each egg.

Sift spices and flour together and add alternately with buttermilk to which baking soda has been added. Add walnuts, jam and vanilla, mixing thoroughly.

Bake in 4 9-inch round greased pans at 350 degrees for 30-35 minutes or until done.

Cake filling:

7 egg yolks
2 cups seedless raisins
1 cup butter
2 cups chopped pecans
2 cups sugar
2 cups coconut, grated
1 cup whipping cream
1 tsp vanilla

Cream softened butter and sugar thoroughly and add egg yolks, blending. Combine mixture with rest of ingredients, except coconut and vanilla.

Cook until thickened, then add coconut and vanilla. Spread between layers and on top and sides.

Southern Breeze Cheesecake

1 package 8-ounce crème cheese, softened
1/3 cup sugar
1 cup sour cream
2 teaspoons vanilla
8 ounces of Cool Whip
1 Graham cracker pie crust
½ cup fresh, sliced strawberries

Beat cheese until smooth, gradually beat in sugar and then blend in the sour cream and vanilla. Fold in the whipped topping and blend well. Then spoon into pie crust.

Chill until set (about 4 hours) and garnish with fresh strawberries.

(My sister **Marcelle Young**)

Frosty Strawberry Squares

1 cup flour
¼ cup brown sugar
½ to 1 cup chopped pecans
½ cup melted butter

Stir together and spread evenly in shallow pan. Bake at 350 degrees for 20 minutes, stirring occasionally. Then sprinkle 2/3 of the crumbs into a 9 x 13 x 2 inch pan.

2 egg whites
1½ cup sugar
2 cups sliced strawberries
1 tablespoon lemon juice
1 8-ounce tub of Cool whip

Combine egg whites, sugar, berries, and lemon juice in large bowl. Beat at high speed until stiff peaks form, about 10 minutes.

Fold in Cool Whip.

Cover crumbs in pan with filling and top with remaining crumbs. Freeze and cut in squares (10-12 servings).

White Cake

2¼ cup flour
1½ cup sugar
1//2 cup shortening
1½ teaspoon vanilla
3¼ teaspoon baking powder
1 teaspoon salt
1 cup milk
4 egg whites

Mix ingredients until batter is smooth, then bake for 20 minutes at 325-350 degrees.

My grandson Jonathan enjoying Frozen French Pastry

FROZEN FRENCH PASTRY

1 1/3 stick margarine or butter
4 whole eggs (beaten)
1 pound box powdered sugar
1 box vanilla wafers
1 cup chopped nuts
1 large container frozen sliced strawberries (about 10 ounces)
1 large can (no larger than 20 ounces) crushed pineapple
2 half-pints whipping cream

STEP 1: Make praline syrup by combining 1 stick of margarine, four whole eggs, and 1 pound of powdered sugar in top of double boiler. Cook for 11/2 hours (uncovered). Stir occasionally, but check often so it will not overcook.

STEP 2: Crush vanilla wafers, add nuts and 1/3 stick melted margarine. Mix together and spread in bottom of a 9 x 12-inch container (reserve 1 cup of crumbs to sprinkle on top).

Pour syrup over crumbs, cover tightly, and place in freezer to chill.

STEP 3: Fold frozen strawberries and crushed pineapple (well drained and chilled) into whipping cream.

Mix well and pour over syrup layer. Sprinkle with crumbs and freeze.

When ready to eat, slice in squares at least ½ hour before serving.

Meringue Kisses

2 egg whites
1/8 teas. Salt
1/8 cup sugar
½ teaspoon vanilla extract

Beat egg whites, gradually adding all other ingredients. Beat until thick enough to drop on cookie sheet lined with brown paper.

Bake at 300 degrees for 25 minutes. Let cool. Carefully transfer to serving dish.

(**Nettie Scruggs**)

Seven Minute Cake Frosting

2 egg whites
1 ½ cup sugar (granulated)
1/3 cup water
2 teas white Karo
Dash of salt
1 teas vanilla

Mix all ingredients except vanilla.

Beat constantly over boiling water in double boiler for about 7 minutes.

Add vanilla and spread over cake.

Dressing for Fruit Salad

½ cup sugar
1 cup pineapple juice
1 tablespoons flour
1 teas butter
1 egg
1 cup whipped topping

Beat all ingredients together and cook on low heat until think.

Cool and fold in whipped topping.

Chill until ready to eat.

Vanilla Wafer Cake

1 12-ounce package of vanilla wafers
1 7-ounce package of Angle Flake coconut
2 sticks of margarine
½ cup sweet milk
2 cups sugar
1 cup chopped pecans

Cream margarine and sugar.

Add eggs, one at a time.

Add all other ingredients.

Bake in tube pan 1 ½ to 2 hours at 275 degrees.

Chess Squares

Chess Squares

1 box yellow cake mix
1 stick margarine
1 egg, beaten

Combine above and pack in 9 x 13 pan.

Topping:
3 eggs, beaten
1 8-ounce cream cheese
1 box powdered sugar
1 teaspoon vanilla

Mix topping mixture and spread over cake mixture.

Bake at 350 degrees for about 45 minutes.

Let cool, and cut in small squares. If you would like to have strawberry or chocolate chess squares, then simply substitute strawberry or chocolate cake mix for the yellow cake mix.

Pecan Puffs

½ cup butter
¼ cup sugar
1 teaspoon vanilla
1 cup sifted cake flour
1 cup nuts
A pinch of salt

Mix butter, sugar, salt and vanilla with mixer at low speed until light and fluffy. Beat in nuts and flour until well mixed. Chill until easy to handle. Pre-heat oven to 350 degrees. Form into balls and spoon onto ungreased baking sheet. Cook 20 minutes at 350 degrees.

Nana's Surprise Pudding

2 eggs
1½ cup sugar
2/3 cup flour
1 ½ teaspoon baking powder
¼ teaspoon salt

Beat above ingredients well in order as given.

Then add 1 cup apples and 1 cup nuts, both chopped. Then add 1 teaspoon vanilla.

Pour into 9-inch greased pan.

Cook at 325 degrees for about 45 minutes.

(Nana Turner)

Chocolate Chess Pie

1 ½ cups sugar
2 tablespoons cocoa
1 stick butter
3 eggs, beaten
1 tablespoon corn meal
1 teaspoon vanilla
1 small can evaporated milk

Melt butter in pan, then add cocoa and all other ingredients. Stir, then pour into 9-inch unbaked pie shell.

Cook at 325 degrees for 45 minutes.

Diane's Easy Peach Cobbler

1 stick margarine
1 large can of peaches and juice

Heat above to boiling point

In a large baking dish, mix well the following:

1 cup self-rising flour
1 cup sugar
1 cup milk

Pour hot mixture over this and back at 350 degrees for about 45 minutes.

Toasted Pecans

½ cup butter
4 cups pecan halves
4 teaspoons Worcestershire sauce
½ teaspoon Tabasco sauce
1 tablespoon garlic salt

Melt butter in pan and add seasonings. Coat pecans with above seasonings. Spread on large flat pan and back at 300 degrees for 30 minutes.

Drain on paper towel or brown paper.

(My daughter **Susan Richardson**)

Me with my daughter Susan

Applesauce Fruit Cake

1 cup butter
1 cup chopped raisins
1 ½ cups sugar
½ cup chopped dates
2 teaspoons cinnamon
½ cup chopped figs
1 teaspoon cloves
½ cup mixed candied fruit
1 teaspoon allspice
½ cup chopped nuts
3 cups flour
2 eggs
½ teaspoon salt
2 cups applesauce
1 ½ teaspoons baking soda

Cream butter and add sugar gradually with spices, creaming until light. Sift flour, salt and soda together. Dredge fruit and nuts in ½ cup of the flour.

Beat eggs until light and add alternately with the remaining of the flour stirring until well blended. Stir in dredged fruits and nuts, and the applesauce.

Bake in a greased tube pan in a slow oven (325 degrees) and 1 ½ hours or until done.

(**Hattie Webb**, my sister-in-law)

Cream Cheese Icing

8 ounce package of cream cheese
1 stick of margarine
1 lb. box of powdered sugar
1 teaspoon of vanilla

Let cream cheese and butter soften.

Beat until creamy, then gradually fold in sugar and vanilla.

Spread on cool cake.

Microwave Banana Pudding

Mix together

2 cups water
2 tablespoons margarine
2 slightly beaten eggs
1 teaspoon vanilla
1/3 cup flour
1 can sweetened condensed milk

Pour 2 ¼ cup boiling water over mixture.

Microwave 1 minute at a time, stirring each time to evaluate consistency.

Once it stirs like pudding should, then add 1 or 2 sliced bananas.

Delicious warm or after being refrigerated.

Once chilled it is tasty with Cool Whip or whipping cream spread on top.

Scalloped Pineapple

4 cups fresh bread crumbs
1 20-ounce can crushed pineapple, drained
3 eggs, beaten
2 cups sugar
1 cup margarine, melted

Toss together break crumbs and pineapple.

Combine other ingredients and pour over pineapple.

Pour over pineapple.

Bake at 350 degrees for 30 minutes

Dot's Orange Cake

1 package cake mix
2/3 cup vegetable oil
4 eggs
½ cup water
1 package orange Jello

Combine ingredients in a bowl and stir until well mixed.

Transfer mixture to a 9-inch baking pan or into a rectangular pan of the type you might use for a pound cake.

Bake at the temperature listed on the cake mix and for the recommended time.

Karo Pecan (or Walnut) Pie

3 eggs, beaten
¼ cup margarine, melted
1 cup white Karo corn syrup
1 tablespoon corn meal
1 cup sugar
1 cup pecans or walnuts, chopped

Mix ingredients, walnuts last.

Pour in unbaked 9-inch pie crust.

Bake at 350 degrees over 50 minutes to 1 hour.

Note: if pie is browning too fast, I make a tent of foil over the pie for the last 15 minutes.

Strawberry Cake

1 box white cake mix
1 small box of strawberry Jello (dry)
4 eggs
1 cup of cooking oil
½ cup water
½ small package of frozen sliced strawberries, thawed with juice from berries
Bake in 9 x 13 pan
Ice when cake cools

Icing
1 box powdered sugar
1 stick of margarine, melted
½ box of frozen sliced strawberries

(Diane Bagley)

Chocolate Sheath Cake

2 cups flour mixed with 2 cups sugar
In a sauce pan, melt:
1 stick butter
2 tablespoons cocoa
1 cup water
Dash of salt
½ cup shortening

When this starts to boil, pour over dry ingredients, then add ½ cup buttermilk with 1 teaspoon baking soda.

Add 2 eggs and 1 teaspoon vanilla.

Pour into 9 x 13 pan.

Bake 25 minutes at 400 degrees.

ICING
1 stick margarine
2 tablespoons cocoa
6 tablespoons milk

When this comes to a boil, add 1 box powdered sugar, then vanilla and nuts.

Spread on cake when it comes out of oven and is still hot.

(Marguerite Haley)

Easy Coconut Cake

1 box deluxe white cake mix
3 eggs
1/3 cup cooking oil
1 ¼ cups water

Mix together, pour into 9x13 pan and bake at 350 degrees for 25 to 30 minutes.

Punch holes in cake with fork, then drizzle 1 can sweetened condensed milk over cake.

Cool, the spread 1 medium carton of Cool Whip, then frozen coconut, 1 cup or more.

This cake must be kept in refrigerator.

(My sister **Marcelle Young**)

Lemon Icebox Pie

1 can sweetened condensed milk
3 egg yoks (save whites for meringue)
1/3 cup lemon juice
1 or 2 cups Cool Whip.
1 graham cracker pie shell

In a 2 quart mixing bowl combine milk and egg yokes. Beat well. Then stir in lemon juice a little at a time. Be sure the above is mixed well, gently spoon in Cool Whip. Spread meringue on pie careful to connect with crust. Brown lightly. Cool and slice in 6 pieces.

Variation: Add sliced strawberries to pie filling before adding the meringue.

Five Flavor Pound Cake

2 sticks butter
½ cup shortening
3 cups sugar
5 eggs, beaten
3 cups all-purpose flour
½ teaspoon baking powder
1 cup milk

1 teaspoon each of:
Vanilla extract
Coconut extract
Rum extract
Lemon extract
Butter extract

Cream butter, shortening and sugar well

Add eggs and beat well

Add mixture of flour and baking powder, alternating with milk. Stir in flavorings

Pour batter in 10 inch tube pan.

Bake at 325 degrees for 1 ½ hours or bake in two loaf pans for about 1 hour. Let cool before turning out on rack to cool

Variation: glaze, if desired
1 cup sugar
½ cup water

1 teaspoon each of the above extracts. Boil mixture until sugar melts. Pour over hot cake in pan. Let cake cool before removing from pan.

(Kay Ingram)

My late companion Angel

Date Nut Cake

1 cup all-purpose flour
½ teaspoon baking powder
½ teaspoon salt
1 cup sugar
4 eggs (separated)
1 lb. chopped dates
1 lb. chopped pecans
½ lb. melted butter
1 teaspoon vanilla

Mix nuts and dates with dry ingredients. Fold in butter, egg yolks and then egg whites. Bake in 2 medium loaf pans at 350 degrees for 1 hour and 1 ¼ hours.

Variation: add 1 cup maraschino cherries. Keep this cake wrapped tightly in alum foil and it will keep well.

Apple Nut Coffee Cake

1 cup flour
½ teaspoon baking powder
½ teaspoon baking soda

½ cup sugar
¼ cup shortening
1 egg
½ teaspoon vanilla

1 apple, chopped
½ cup sour cream

¼ cup nuts, crushed
¼ cup brown sugar
1 tablespoon butter
½ teaspoon cinnamon

Grease and flour 8-inch cake pan.

Mix first three ingredients.

Cream sugar, shortening, egg and vanilla.

Add dry ingredients. Mix in apple and sour cream.

Pour into pan, top with last 4 ingredients.

Bake at 350 degrees for 25 to 30 minutes.

(Ruth Benton)

Peanut Butter Pie

1 cookie pie crust
1 ounces cream cheese
½ cup peanut butter
1 cup powdered sugar
8 ounces Cool Whip
Chocolate syrup to taste

Mix all together into a bowl and pour into crust.

Keep in refrigerator or freeze.

Toasted Coconut Pie

3 eggs, beaten
½ cup margarine, melted
1 teaspoon vanilla
1 cup sugar
4 teaspoons lemon juice
1 small can coconut

Mix all ingredients, pour in unbaked pie crust, and bake at 350 degrees for 40-45 minutes.

Three-Layer Banana Cake

2½ cups sugar
1 cup butter
3 cups flour
4 eggs
2 teaspoons baking soda into 8 teaspoons buttermilk
2 teaspoons vanilla
2 cups mashed bananas

Cream butter and sugar. Add all other ingredients., except bananas. Mix well, then add bananas. Bake at 350 degrees.

FILLING:
Cream together the following:
1½ box confectioners sugar
½ cup butter
½ cup mashed bananas
Pecans

Honeybun Cake

1 box yellow cake mix
4 eggs
¾ cup vegetable oil
8 ounces sour cream

¾ cup brown sugar
3 tablespoons cinnamon
Milk as needed

Mix above ingredients in bowl. In a separate bowl, mix 3 tablespoons cinnamon with ¾ cup of brown sugar. In an oblong pan, layer ½ cake mixture, ½ cinnamon mixture. Swirl the mixture. Then repeat, ending with cinnamon swirl. Bake at 325 degrees for 45 minutes.

GLAZE:
2 cups powdered sugar
1 teaspoon vanilla
Add milk sparingly to the mixture, stirring as you pour, until you see a glaze take shape. Then pour over warm cake.

Susan's Quick, Easy Candy

Susan's Quick, Easy Candy

1 package vanilla almond bark
1 12-ounce package of chocolate semi-sweet chips
1 jar dry roasted peanuts

Use double boiler and melt first bark bar and then chocolate chips.

All peanuts, mix well.

Using a full tablespoon, drop on wax paper.

Let cool. Store in air-tight tin.

Susan's Lazy Day Cake

Grease oblong baking dish.
Layer in the following order:
1 can cherry pie mix
1 tall can (#2) crushed pineapple, drained
1 package Duncan Hines Deluxe2 Yellow Cake Mix
1 cup chopped pecans
2 sticks melted margarine

Bake at 350 degrees for one hour.
Serve warm or cool with ice cream or topping of your choice.

Coconut Cream Pie

3 egg yolks (save whites for meringue)
1/3 cup flour
1 can sweetened condensed milk
1 cups hot water
¼ stick margarine
1 teaspoon vanilla extract

In a 2-quart glass microwaveable mixing bowl combine first 3 ingredients Beat well, then slowly add hot water. Stir well.

Cook in microwave for 6 minutes at 2-minute intervals.

After the last 2 minutes, add butter, vanilla and ¾ small can or ¾ package of frozen coconut mix well, then spoon in 8-9 inch cooked pastry shell.

Make meringue from saved egg whites.

Spread on pie, then sprinkle coconut on meringue.

Brown in oven.

Cool and cut pie in 6 or 8 pieces.

Meringue for Pies

3 egg whites
6 tablespoons sugar

Beat egg whites until fluffy.

Add sugar 2 tablespoons at a time. Beat after each addition. Continue beating until mixture stands in peaks.

Spoon mixture on pie and spread evenly.

Bake in 425 degree oven for 5 to 10 minutes.

Authentic Southern Pastry

2¼ cup all-purpose flour.
1 teaspoon salt
1 cup shortening
6 tablespoons ice water

Mix flour and salt. Cut in shortening. Add water, 1 tablespoon at a time. If needed, carefully add more water, small amount at a time.

This is a rich, fragile crust and must be handled carefully.

Divide mixture in 2 parts and roll out one at a time. Prick with a fork before baking.

Bake at 425 degrees for 10-12 minutes.

Freshly baked caramel pie

My Favorite Caramel Pie

3 egg yolks (save whites for meringue)
1/3 cup flour
1 can sweetened condensed milk
2 cups hot water
½ cup sugar
¼ stick butter
1 teaspoon vanilla extract

In an iron skillet, slowly—and I stress the word slowly because it can burn before you know it—brown the sugar, then pour in hot water and set mixture aside.

In a 2-quart glass microwavable mixing bowl combine first three ingredients. Beat well.

Then gradually add water with brown sugar in it. Stir well.

Cook in microwave for 6 minutes at 2 minute intervals, stirring after each time. After last 2 minutes add butter and vanilla. Sit. Then spoon into cooked 8 by 9 inch pie crust.

Make meringue from saved egg whites and spread on pie.

Brown in oven.

Cool, and cut into 8 or 9 slices when served.

Apple Cobbler

½ cup margarine
2 cups sugar
2 cups water
1 ½ cups sifted flour
½ cup milk
2 cups finely chopped apples
1 teaspoon cinnamon
Heat oven to 350 degrees.
Melt butter in 13 x 9 backing dish

In a saucepan heat sugar and water until sugar melts.

Cut shortening into flour until fine. Add milk and stir with fork only until dough leaves the side of the bowl.

Transfer dough to lightly floured board, knead just until smooth. Roll dough into large rectangle ¼ inch thick. Sprinkle cinnamon over apples then pour apples over the dough.

Roll dough like jelly roll and seal.

Slice dough into 16 slices ½ inches thick. Place in pan with melted butter. Pour sugary syrup around rolls. Crust will absorb liquid.

Bake at 350 degrees for 1 hour.

(My sister **Marcelle Young**)

Pumpkin Ice Cream Pie

1 package instant vanilla pudding mix
1 can (16 ounce) pumpkin
½ cup milk
1 teaspoon pumpkin pie spice
1pint vanilla ice cream, softened
1 9-inch, graham cracker pie shell
Whipped cream and nuts

Combine mix, pumpkin, milk and spice.

Mix with mixer at low speed for 1 minute, well blended.

Add ice cream and beat until well mixed.

Cool and serve.

(My sister **Marcelle Young**)

Heavenly Hash

1 8½-ounce cup of pineapple
2 cups Cool Whip
1 Cup coconut
 Cup miniature marshmallows
¼ cup chopped maraschino cherries
3 tablespoons of milk
Mix and chill

(My sister **Marcelle Young**)

Buttermilk Pound Cake

1 cup butter
3 cups sugar
5 egg yoks (well beaten)
1 cup buttermilk
3 cups of flour
5 egg whites (beaten)
1/3 teaspoon baking soda dissolved in buttermilk
2 teaspoons vanilla
Powdered sugar (sprinkled as directed)

Cream butter and sugar, add egg yoks, flour and milk. Next blend in egg whites and vanilla.

Pour in greased Bundt pan that has been dusted in powdered sugar.

Cook at 325 degrees for 1 hour and 10 minutes or until fork inserted into cake comes out clean.

Cool.

Sprinkle powdered sugar.

Good sliced and toasted.

My son James and I in the 1990s

Old Fashioned Delta Ice Cream

8 eggs
2½ cups sugar
½ gallon milk
1 pint whipping cream
2 teaspoons vanilla

Mix eggs, sugar and milk until smooth. Cook in double boiler until the mixture thickens.

Add whipping cream and vanilla to the mixture and freeze in one large container or several smaller containers of your choice.

(My sister **Marcelle Young**)

Delta Fig Cake

2 cups all-purpose flour
3 eggs
1 teaspoon cinnamon
1 cup cooking oil
1 teaspoon cloves
1 cup buttermilk
1 teaspoon nutmeg
1½ cups sugar
1 teaspoon salt
1 cup fig preserves, chopped
1 teaspoon baking soda
1 teaspoon on baking soda
1 teaspoon vanilla

Mix all dry ingredients, add oil and beat well. Add eggs, one at a time, alternating with milk, than add figs, vanilla, and pecans. Bake in pan at 350 degrees for 1 hour.

Sauce for Fig Cake

1 cup sugar
½ cup buttermilk
1 teaspoon vanilla
1 tablespoon white corn syrup
½ teaspoon baking soda
½ to 1 stick butter or margarine

Bake all ingredients for 3 minutes, stirring constantly.

Pour over cake and let cake cool in pan.

(Dot Peyton)

Mississippi Mud Cake

2 sticks margarine
1 cup Angel Flake coconut
1 ½ cup flour, sifted
2 cups sugar
1 ½ cup chopped pecans
2 tablespoons cocoa
4 eggs
1 teaspoon vanilla

Mix and spread in 9 x 13 pan. Bake at 350 degrees for 30 minutes or until done. While hot spread on a large jar of marshmallow crème. Let cool and ice with the following:

1 box powdered sugar
½ cup cocoa
1 teaspoon vanilla
½ cup margarine
½ cup Pet milk

Whipping Cream Pound Cake

½ lb. butter
3 cups sugar
6 eggs
3 cups cake flour
1 carton whipping cream (1/2 pint)
2 teaspoons vanilla missed with above ingredients

Cream butter and sugar well. Add eggs one at a time, beating well after each addition. Add flour, alternating with whipping cream.

Start in cold oven set at 325 degrees, and cook 1 ½ hours.

Hummingbird Cake

3 cups flour
¼ cup vegetable oil
1 tsp baking soda
1½ teaspoons vanilla
½ teaspoon salt
1 8-ounce can crushed pineapple, undrained
2 cups sugar
1teaspoon ground cinnamon
1 cup chopped pecans
3 eggs, beaten
1¾ cup mashed bananas

Combine first 5 ingredients in large bowl and add eggs, oil (stirring until dry ingredients are moistened. DO NOT BEAT))

Stir in vanilla, pineapple, 1 cup pecans, and bananas.

Pour into 3 greased and flour-dusted 9-inch cake pans. Bake at 350 degrees for 23 to 38 minutes or until done. Cool in pan.

Frosting:
Make certain cake has completely cooled before frosting.
1 cup margarine, softened
1 8-ounce package of cream cheese
1 16-ouncwe package of powdered sugar, sifted
1 teaspoon of vanilla

Cream margarine and cream cheese. Then gradually add powdered sugar. Beat until mixture is light and fluffy. Stir in vanilla and ½ cup chopped nuts.

Here I am adjusting Susan's wedding veil

Rum Cake

1 package yellow cake mix (Duncan Hines Deluxe)
1 package instant Jello pudding (vanilla)
4 whole eggs
½ cup vegetable oil
½ cup light rum
½ cup cold water

Combine ingredients and put mixture into electric mixer and beat a full 10 minutes at medium speed (very important)

Bake in greased and floured tube pan. Sprinkle chopped nut (heavy layer of nuts works best) in bottom of pan before you put batter in pan

Bake at 325 degrees for 1 hour

While still warm in the pan, pour the following mixture over the cake:

1 cup sugar
½ cup butter or margarine (1 stick)
¼ cup water

Boil one minute and remove from heat

After it cools slightly add ¼ cup of light rum

Pour this mixture over cake while still warm and leave in pan to cool

Vola's Sock It to Me Cake

1 box Duncan Hines Supreme cake mix
1 box sour cream
¾ cup butter
¾ cup butter flavored vegetable oil
4 eggs

Mix cake mix, sour cream and vegetable oil. Then add 1 egg at a tie, mixing well after each addition. Pour half the batter into the greased tube pan and add the following mixture:
2 teaspoon cinnamon
½ cup light brown sugar
½ cup nuts

Add the remaining batter and bake at 325 degrees for about 1 hour
Topping:
½ box confectionary sugar
1 teaspoon vanilla
½ stick margarine
2 or 3 tablespoons of sweet milk

(**Vola** was my father's second wife)

Prune Cake

1 cup salad oil
3 eggs
1 ½ cup sugar
2 cups flour
1 cup buttermilk
1 cup chopped nuts
1 cup cooked prunes, drained and chopped
¼ teaspoon salt
1 teaspoon baking soda
1 teaspoon cinnamon
1 teaspoon nutmeg
1 teaspoon all spice
1 teaspoon vanilla

Blend sugar and eggs, adding oil. Sift dry ingredients and add alternately with buttermilk, vanilla, nuts and prunes.

Bake at 300 degrees for 50 minutes in 9 x 13 tube pan.

Buttermilk Glaze Topping:

2 cups sugar
¾ cup buttermilk
½ teaspoon baking soda
1 tablespoon corn syrup
1/4 cup margarine
1 teaspoon vanilla

Mix all together and cook until soft.

Let cool, stir and pour on cake.

My sister Marcelle and I. We were more than sisters, we were best friends

Swedish Pecan Balls

1 cup ground pecans
2 tablespoons sugar
½ cup butter or margarine
1 cup flour
1 teaspoon vanilla
1/8 teaspoon salt
Powdered sugar

Combine all ingredients except powdered sugar. Shape dough into balls the size of walnuts. Place on ungreased cookie sheet.

Bake at 275 degrees for 30 minutes. Roll in powdered sugar while hot. Makes two dozen.

Cream Caramel Cake

2 sticks butter
3 cups sugar
6 eggs
1 teaspoon vanilla
2 2/3 cups all-purpose flour
¼ teaspoon baking soda
1 teaspoon salt
1 8-ounce carton of sour cream

Preheat oven to 350 degrees.
Cream butter and sugar, and add eggs one at a time.
Sift flour, baking soda and salt, alternating.
Add flour and sour cream to butter mixture. Add vanilla.
Pour into 3 9-inch pans.
Bake 25-35 minutes or undone done.
Cool on racks for 10 minutes'
Remove cake from pan and cool

FROSTING:
½ lb. butter
2 cups dark brown sugar
½ can evaporated milk
4 cups confectionary sugar
1 teaspoon vanilla

Melt butter, add brown sugar and milk. Cook 2 minutes over medium heat, stirring constantly. Remove from heat. Add vanilla and pour over confectionary sugar. Beat until smooth.

Let cool slightly, then frost the layers, top and sides.

Here my daughter Susan and I are starting out on our trip to Washington, D.C. in 1955. Sixty-four years later in 2019 we are still on a journey of discovery.

Sweet Potato Cake

1½ cup vegetable oil
2 cups sugar
4 eggs, separated
4 tablespoons hot water
2½ cups self-rising flour
1 tablespoon cinnamon
1 tablespoon nutmeg
1 tablespoon vanilla
1 cup nuts 1½ cup grated raw sweet potatoes

Mix oil and sugar and beat until smooth. Then add egg yoks, beat well and add hot water and dry ingredients which should have been sifted together.

Stir in potatoes, nuts, and vanilla.

Fold in stiffly beaten egg whites.

Bake in sheath cake pan at 350 degrees for 25 to 30 minutes.

Cake Filling:
1 large can evaporated milk
1 cup sugar
1 stick margarine
3 egg yoks
1 tablespoon vanilla
11/3 cup coconut

Combine all ingredients, except the coconut. Cook over medium heat for 12 minutes. Add coconut and stir until cool. Spread on top of cake. Keep in covered container.

Bridge was always a way of life in the Mississippi Delta.
Here I am, third from left, with my friends
Left to right, Adrene Hollingsworth, my best friend Dot Peyton, who was
celebrating her birthday, and Rivers Catledge

Bess Truman's Ozark Pudding

2 eggs, well beaten
1½ cup sugar
Beat well, then add:
2/3 cup flour
2 ½ teaspoons baking powder
¼ teaspoon salt
Again, beat well, then add:
1 cup chopped apple
1 cup chopped nuts
1 tablespoon vanilla

Bake in greased pan at 325 degrees for about 45 minutes to 1 hour. Allow to cool and enjoy.

This is one of my favorite recipes.

Italian Cream Cake
(3 layer)

1 stick butter
½ cup Crisco oil (or substitute)
2 cups sugar
5 egg yolks
2 cups cake flour
21 cup chopped nuts
5 egg whites
1 teaspoon baking soda
1 cup buttermilk
1 teaspoon vanilla
1 can of coconut

Cream margarine and Crisco, adding sugar while creaming egg yoks. Sift flour and baking soda together. Add flour mixtures, alternating with buttermilk. Add vanilla, coconut and nuts. Fold In beaten egg whites and bake at 325 degrees for 30 minutes.

ICING:
 8 ounces of softened cream cheese
1/3 stick of softened margarine
1 box confectionary sugar
1 teaspoon vanilla

Mix together.

Smooth out each layer and top.

You can sprinkle the top with coconut or nuts

Cherry-Oatmeal Cookies

½ cup shortening
½ cup margarine
¾ cup brown sugar
½ cup granulated sugar
2 teaspoons all spice
¼ teaspoon baking soda
¼ teaspoon salt
2 eggs
1 teaspoon vanilla
1 1/3 cups all-purpose flour
2 ½ cups rolled oats
1 ½ cups dried cherries
1 teaspoon grated orange peel

Cream margarine and shortening.

Add sugar, granulated sugar, all spice, baking soda, and salt.

Beat until fluffy. Then add eggs and vanilla, beat well. Add flour and beat well. Stir in cherries and orange peel.

Fill 1/3 measuring cup with dough and drop on creased cookie sheet, placing cookies three inches apart.

Bake at 375 degrees for 8 to 10 minutes, or until edges are golden brown.

Let stand 1 minute, then transfer to wire rack. Store cookies in air-tight container up to 3 days or freeze up to 3 months.

Makes 14 large cookies.

Here I am in 2019 meeting my son's cocker spaniel, Charlie, for the first time. It was love at first sight for all involved.

Boston Cream Pie (single loaf)

1/3 cup shortening
1 cup sugar
2 eggs
¾ cup milk
1 teaspoon vanilla
1 ¼ cup un-sifted all-purpose flour
½ teaspoon baking soda
¼ teaspoon salt

Cream shortening, sugar, eggs and vanilla until light and fluffy. Combine ingredients with milk to creamed mixture. Pour batter into well-greased and lightly floured 9-inch cake pan. Bake at 350 degrees for 30 to 35 minutes.

FILLING:
1/3 cup sugar
2 tablespoons cornstarch
1 ½ cups of milk
2 eggs, beaten
1 tablespoon butter
1 teaspoon vanilla

Dissolve cornstarch and sugar in eggs, beat and add milk slowly. Cook in double boiler until thick. Cool and spread between cooled cake layers. Top with glaze if desired.

GLAZE:
3 tablespoons water
2 tablespoons butter
3 tablespoons cocoa
1 cup confectionary sugar
½ teaspoon of vanilla

German Chocolate Cake
(3 layer cake)

1 cup cocoa
2 cups sugar
1 cup shortening (or 1 stick butter or margarine)
4 egg yolks
1 cup buttermilk
1 teaspoon baking soda
21/2 cups flour
1 teaspoon vanilla
½ cup very hot water
4 eggs
3 9-inch baking pans
Dash of salt

For starters, you should know that German Chocolate Cake is *not* a product of Germany. The cake gets its name from German's Sweet Chocolate, a brand of chocolate sold by the Baker Chocolate Company (now Kraft Foods). The chocolate was created by a fellow named Sam German. The cake is much sweeter than the traditional chocolate cake, which is probably why it has always been so popular in the Mississippi Delta, where sweetness is a prime characteristic of favored desserts for family gatherings or church events.

To begin, mix the cocoa and hot water in a bowl, stirring well before setting the bowl aside. Next, cream shortening, sugar and vanilla into a bowl and beat it until it is somewhat fluffy. Then add egg one at a time, beating the mixture after each egg is added.

Next, stir the flour, baking soda, and salt together. Then add the butter mixture, alternately adding the chocolate mixture and the buttermilk, using a rubber spatula to blend the ingredients. Bake in greased, round 9-inch cake pans for 25 minutes at 350 degrees. While barely warm, cover with icing.

140

ICING
1 can sweetened condensed milk
3 egg yolks, beaten
½ cup butter or margarine
1 teaspoon vanilla
1 1/3 cups sweet coconut flakes
1 cup pecan or walnut halves

Stir the sweetened condensed milk, butter and egg yolks in a saucepan, cooking over low heat, being careful to stir almost constantly until the mixture is bubbling and visually thickened. Remove from heat and stir in vanilla, coconut and nuts. Allow to cool to room temperature. This makes almost 3 cups of icing.

Caramel Brownies

1 14-ounce package of Kraft caramels
2/3 cup evaporated milk
1 package German chocolate cake mix
¾ cup of melted margarine
1 cup chopped nuts
1 16-ounce package of chocolate chips

Combine the caramels with 1/3 cup of evaporated milk and cook over low heat until all is melted. Grease and lightly flour 9 x 13 pan. In a large bowl combine dry cake mix, butter, 1/3 cup evaporated milk, and nuts. Stir and then spoon about 2/3 of the mixture into the pan, reserving the remaining mixture for topping.
Bake at 350 degrees for 6 minutes.
For topping, sprinkle chocolate chips over crust. Spread caramel mixture over chips. Crumble remaining dough over caramel. Bake at 350 degrees for 15 to 18 minutes.
Needs to cool before it is served.

(my daughter **Susan Richardson**)

Our Favorite Recipes

Janet Young, my sister Marcelle's youngest daughter
"Any of the fruit cobblers in this book"
Peach Cobbler Page 101, Apple Cobbler, page 120

Martha, McKernan, my sister Marcelle's oldest daughter
Amalgamation Cake, Page 91
Fried Quail, Page 61

Emily McCaskill, my great grand-daughter
Meringue Kisses
Page 96

Zachary Freyre, my great grandson
Strawberry Cake
Page 106

Ashlyn McLendon, my great grand-daughter
Sweet Potato Casserole
Page 13

Aiden McLendon, my great grand-son
Pecan Pie
Page 106

Suzie Duke, my great grand-daughter
Sourdough Bread
Page 51

CPSIA information can be obtained
at www.ICGtesting.com
Printed in the USA
BVHW070125070319
542021BV00007B/31/P